Discover India

MOUNTAINS AND RIVERS OF INDIA

Sonia Mehta

PUFFIN BOOKS
An imprint of Penguin Random House

PUFFIN BOOKS

USA | Canada | UK | Ireland | Australia | New Zealand | India | South Africa | China

Puffin Books is part of the Penguin Random House group of companies
whose addresses can be found at global.penguinrandomhouse.com

Published by Penguin Random House India Pvt. Ltd
4th Floor, Capital Tower 1, MG Road,
Gurugram 122 002, Haryana, India

First published in Puffin Books by Penguin Random House India 2022

Text, design and illustrations copyright © Quadrum Solutions Pvt. Ltd 2022
Series copyright © Penguin Random House India 2022

Picture Credits
P 13: Badrinath, Uttarakhand (Nila Newsom/Shutterstock.com); P 32: Alleppey Backwaters, Kerala (CRS PHOTO/Shutterstock.com);
P 34: View of Chenab River (Arun Sambhu Mishra/Shutterstock.com); P 38: Haridwar, Uttarakhand (Stocksvids/Shutterstock.com);
P 43: Gomti Ghat and Hindu Temple 'Shree Dwarkadhish' (Imagine Rural/Shutterstock.com); P 43: River Kosi (Bodom/Shutterstock.com);
P 44: River Brahmaputra, Assam North East (Hari Mahidhar/Shutterstock.com); P 46: Mishing tribal village house at Majuli Island
(Abhilekh Saikia/Shutterstock.com); P 48: Hooghly River at dusk time in Kolkata, West Bengal (Hari Mahidhar/Shutterstock.com);
P 48: Container ship in Ganga River (S B Stock/Shutterstock.com); P 49: Howrah Bridge, Kolkata (Mayank Makhija/Shutterstock.com);
P 50: Aerial view of Statue of Unity (Kunal Mahto/Shutterstock.com); P 55: Ramkund or Panchavati, ghat on the sacred river Godavari
(tantrik71/Shutterstock.com); P 60: Periyar National Park and Wildlife Sanctuary (Vishal Gulati/Shutterstock.com);
P 60: Tribals fishing in the Periyar River (Sids/Shutterstock.com)

ISBN 9780143455370

Design and layout by Quadrum Solutions Pvt. Ltd
Printed at Aarvee Promotions, India

www.penguin.co.in

Hello Kids!

I'm so happy you are reading this book. India is an incredible country, and there are lots of things about it that we don't know.

I discovered India because my father was in the Indian army. He was posted to many places all over India, and we dutifully followed him. Can you imagine that by the time I was in the tenth standard, I had changed nine schools? Of course it was hard making new friends almost every year, but the good part was that I got to live in so many places. Right from Kerala, where I was born, to Kashmir, Jhansi, Shillong, Chandigarh, Goa . . . the list is long.

I remember our home in Shillong. It was on the edge of a cliff called Happy Valley. Seeing the soaring mountains from the veranda of our house was a sight that I'll never forget. And when we lived in Goa, I remember crossing the river on a ferry to get to school every day. What wonderful mountains and rivers we have in India! It's what made me write this book.

I do hope you enjoy this visit to India's mountains and rivers and get a sense of how vast and spectacular they are. And that you enjoy reading this book as much as I have enjoyed writing it. I would love to hear from you. So do write to me at sonia.mehta@quadrumltd.com.

Lots of love,
Sonia Aunty

Mishki and Pushka have come to visit Earth from their home planet, Zoomba. They have never seen such an amazing place. Zoomba doesn't have trees and mountains and rivers like Earth does. But the people look exactly the same. When they come to Earth, they meet a sweet old man whom they call Daadu Dolma. Daadu Dolma shows them all the wonderful places in India and tells Mishki and Pushka all about them.

Mishki and Pushka can't believe what they see. They have seen many wondrous places on Earth, but they have never, ever seen a place like India.

Get set to explore India with Daadu Dolma, Mishki and Pushka.

Mishki

Mishki is a curious little girl. She is always asking loads of questions. On her home planet, she is always getting into trouble for poking her nose into things that are not her business.

Pushka

Pushka is Mishki's brother. He loves adventure. He is always ready for a new challenge. Whether it's climbing a mountain, or diving into a cold, cold sea, he is up for it.

Daadu Dolma

Daadu Dolma is a wise old man who has lived on Earth longer than the mountains and the seas. No one quite knows how old he is, but what's certain is that he knows everything about everything.

Mishki and Pushka have been thinking. 'Daadu,' says Pushka, 'while we have seen so much of India and its states, something that struck me is that there seem to be an enormous amount of mountains and hills everywhere. Would you say India is a mountainous country?'

'No, Pushka,' replies Daadu. 'Though it has many mountains—some of the largest in the world too—it also has massive plains, plateaus and even deserts.'

'And rivers,' adds Mishki. 'You forgot the rivers, Daadu.'

'Well, yes. I was coming to that,' agrees Daadu, smiling. 'People in India consider their rivers to be religious. In fact, rivers play a huge role not only in the lives of people but also in their culture.'

'Oh! So do you think we can visit some mountains and rivers across India?'

'We certainly can,' Daadu replies. 'Pack your bags and get ready then. And make sure you have some mountain-climbing equipment. There are some pretty tall peaks we can explore.'

Mishki and Pushka hurriedly pack their things. They are off to explore . . .

THE MOUNTAINS AND RIVERS OF INDIA!

A SNEAK PEEK

MOUNTAINS

India's mountains have a massive role to play in the lives of its people. They have stood guard against invaders for centuries, and even given birth to rivers that feed the country. Some truly magnificent wildlife roams in their forests. And guess what? People believe that some of India's several gods have their homes on the icy mountaintops! So getting to know India's mountains is getting to know its history, geography, lifestyle and culture too. Let's get right to it!

All across India

When you think of mountains in India, you think of the Himalayas. Well, they probably *are* the best-known mountain ranges in the world. But apart from the Himalayas, there are multiple ranges spread across the country. It's almost as if they hold the land together—like how bones hold our bodies together.

Let's take a look at all that they do for us.

1. They help rainfall (because as we all know, warm, moisture-filled air pushes up along slopes of mountains and comes down as rain).

2. They give birth to rivers—and without rivers, where would we be?

3. They stop harsh winds from blowing across the land and thereby manage the weather for us.

4. The water that comes crashing down mountainsides helps us generate electricity.

5. Their forests are home to some of the world's most amazing wildlife.

6. They play a crucial role in countering the effects of global warming.

7. They give us sights of majestic beauty and are wonderful places to holiday in.

Jumbled up

Pushka wants to remember why mountains are important. But as always, he's mixed up the words. Can you unscramble them?

1. Mountains give birth to _____. VRERIS

2. They help it _____. NARI

3. Some amazing wild animals live in the _____. RTSFOSE

THE GREAT HIMALAYAS

We simply can't start a discussion on India's mountains without first talking about the Himalayas. And with good reason! The Himalayan range, which spans several parts of Asia, has the world's highest mountains and peaks. The entire range stretches for more than—hold your breath—1500 miles, across Pakistan, Tibet, Nepal, Bhutan and India. Whew! It has over a hundred peaks that are as high as 24,000 feet above sea level. The Indian stretch forms the northernmost border of India, creating a virtually impassable barrier between India and the lands to the north.

Did you know?
The word 'Himalayas' comes from the Sanskrit words hima (snow) and alaya (abode). So it actually means 'where the snow lives'.

Millions of years old

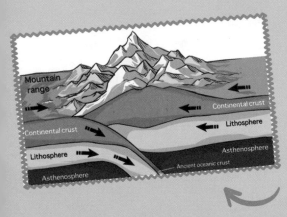

When the earth was first formed, the Himalayas didn't exist as they are today. There were massive landforms and deep waterbodies, shifting and colliding, creating newer landforms. Around 50 million years ago—and that's a really long time— the land that became India collided with the land that is now Eurasia. And over the past 65 million years, powerful forces beneath the earth heaved and pushed, forming the vast number of mountain ranges we call the Himalayas.

An awesome sight!

Steep jagged peaks, soaring cliffs, deep valleys, snow-filled glaciers and deep river gorges— are these what come to mind when you think of the Himalayas? Well, you're quite right. The Himalayas are made of a number of massive mountains with some truly breathtaking peaks. But did you know that all the Himalayas are not snow covered? In fact, the largest parts, especially in India, are below the snow line.

Glaciers galore

There are numerous ice-bound glaciers in the Himalayas that are the birthplaces of some of Asia's most important rivers. The largest of these is the Gangotri, one of the sources of the Ganges. There are other glaciers too that do not fall within the boundaries of India, but which feed its rivers. Sadly, because of global warming, some of these are melting faster than ever before; environmentalists worry that this could cause water crises in the future.

Like a sentry

The Himalayas have stood guard on the northern border of India—just like a sentry does, not allowing invaders to cross easily into India. There have been umpteen attempts to do so all through history. Alexander the Great, the Macedonian emperor, was one of the few who managed to cross into India through the famous Khyber Pass. Over the centuries, intrepid travellers and mountaineers have managed to create more passes, which now pilgrims, travellers and traders use.

Mountains of many parts

The magnificent Himalayas are actually a series of four parallel mountain belts—each quite unique in its own way. If you go from south to north, this is the way you'd see them: first are the outer Himalayas, which are mainly made of the Siwalik range; then come the Lesser or Lower Himalayas; and finally, you come to the Great Himalayas. A large part of the Great Himalayas is in Nepal and Tibet.

State after state

As you can imagine, the Indian Himalayas are not confined to one state. They pass through ten Indian states and union territories. Beginning their journey from Jammu and Kashmir, they make their way through Himachal Pradesh, Uttarakhand, Sikkim, Arunachal Pradesh, Meghalaya, Nagaland, Mizoram, Tripura, Assam and West Bengal. As they go through these states, we begin to understand why the culture in these states is similar to each other in various ways—and also so different from the states in the rest of India.

Forest fables

The Himalayas are so vast and diverse that there are numerous types of landforms within them. You'll find valleys sheltered from harsh winds, snowbound mountains, cliffs and ravines set beside gentle river-fed slopes. So naturally, the vegetation is just as diverse. Depending on how high the area is and how much rain it gets, the vegetation ranges from evergreen forests in the lowest regions, to alpine forests in the higher areas and some fertile low-lying hills in between. So you get to see a vast variety of trees and flowers as you make your way across the Himalayas.

Wildlife wonders

Some lovely wildlife, like snow leopards, brown bears, Tibetan yaks and red pandas, roams the higher reaches of the Himalayas. While in the lower reaches, one would see Asiatic black bears, musk deer, the hangul, langurs and clouded leopards. Several of these are endangered, and environmentalists are doing all they can to preserve them.

Hidden countries

The countries that the Himalayas stretch across are hidden in this grid. Can you find them?

Q	W	E	R	T	Y	U	I	O	P
P	A	K	I	S	T	A	N	X	B
A	S	D	F	G	I	S	E	D	H
Z	X	C	V	B	B	V	B	N	U
E	D	R	F	Y	E	E	R	F	T
D	C	F	V	G	T	E	D	R	A
U	N	E	P	A	L	F	G	H	N
Z	X	S	D	C	V	F	G	B	H
R	T	Y	U	I	I	N	D	I	A

Life in the Himalayas

Numerous mountain tribes make their home in this rugged terrain. Some of these are shepherds who move their flocks to the shelter of the valleys during the harsh winters and then take them back to the higher slopes when summer comes. Tribes like the Gaddi, Gujari, Champa, Ladakhi, Balti, Lepcha, Dard among others, live here. Some migrated centuries ago from China and their culture is very similar to that of Tibet. Others found their way here through Afghanistan, which is why their food and language is similar to Afghani culture. And, of course, a large number are Buddhist, thanks again to the Tibetan influence.

Living with the cold

Brrrr! It ranges from cold to freezing in most parts of the Himalayas. Though styles vary from state to state, most hardcore dwellers wear woollen clothes that are often made from coarse yak wool or sheep wool. While in the higher reaches, people are invariably shepherds, the lower foothills are fabulous for growing tea and fruit. Some of India's loveliest and most productive tea estates are here. And how can we forget the famous Himalayan apples, with the large number of apple orchards that dot the region?

Home sweet home

Because of the valleys, a lot of houses in the Himalayas are built on stilts, which help level them when built on slopes. Traditional homes were built with stone and wood, though now more modern materials like cement and bricks have made an appearance. In several homes, you'll see that tiny windows are built to keep the cold out. In the eastern Himalayas, an area prone to earthquakes, homes are lightweight and often made of bamboo, the most locally available material.

Keeping the faith

There are a whole lot of religious places nestled in the Himalayan mountain ranges that people of different faiths try to visit at least once in their lifetime. These include Mount Kailash in the Tibetan Himalayas, where Shiva is believed to have his abode; the Yamunotri and Gangotri glaciers, where the famous rivers have their origins; Dharamsala, where the Dalai Lama resides; Kedarnath, Badrinath and Rishikesh, which are hotspots for pilgrimages. Millions throng there to pray. Apart from these, there are scores of famous temples sprinkled around the peaks and valleys. There are spectacular Buddhist monasteries too, in the Himalayas.

Oh-so charming!

The mountains provide such bounties of majestic beauty that several towns have sprung up as popular tourist spots. Some of these are charming towns built by the British who went around India looking for places with the cold climate that they had back home. Darjeeling, Dalhousie, Mussoorie, Landour and Shimla are a few places in the Himalayas where the colonial influence is still rather evident.

RANGES AND PEAKS

As we saw, the Himalayas are not a single large mountain, but several small and large ranges and peaks. Here are some of the more prominent ones.

THE SIWALIK RANGE

The stunning Siwalik range is a part of the outer Himalayas. Guess where it gets its name from? Lord Shiva! People believed that Lord Shiva must have lived in the highest parts of this range. It is sandwiched between the higher Himalayas and great river plains and extends across 1600 km. The range is at an average height of between 3000 and 4000 feet above sea level. Its foothills go meandering through Jammu and Kashmir, Himachal Pradesh, Uttarakhand, parts of Punjab, Haryana and Chandigarh. The slopes of the Siwalik range that go down into India's river plains are called a Dun. Dehradun is the most famous of these.

The deposits in the Siwalik range have fossil remains of some African animals like giraffes and hippopotamuses. This tells us how much land must have shifted through millions of years.

THE KARAKORAM RANGE

This range soars at the northernmost tip of India. It's a very important region because the borders of China, Pakistan, India, Afghanistan and Tajikistan all converge amongst the slopes and peaks of this remote area. Its name comes from the Turkic term for 'black rock'. As you can imagine, the terrain is harsh, with craggy rocks and peaks, steep slopes and heavy glaciers. This makes it hard for people to live—which is why it is quite sparsely populated. Gilgit, Leh and Skardu are its largest towns.

THE PIR PANJAL RANGE

Much of the Pir Panjal Range falls in Jammu and Kashmir. Apart from its stunning views, it has some incredible tunnels and passes. The Rohtang Pass, the Haji Pir Pass and the Banihal Pass are some of the famous passes that people have used over centuries. More recently, some tunnels have been created to make travelling in this difficult terrain a little easier.

THE ZANSKAR RANGE

This group of mountains falls mainly in the Jammu and Kashmir territory—spilling into Tibet as well. The Kamet peak, at over 25,000 feet above sea level, is their highest point. The range has some important passes called Shipki, Lipu Lekh and Mana. It also gives birth to multiple small rivers that eventually find their way into the Indus, a river that flows mainly into Pakistan.

Peak performance

Some of the most dramatic peaks in the world are in the Himalayas. Kanchenjunga, a peak that soars at a height of over 28,000 feet above sea level on the border of India and Nepal, is the third highest peak in the world.

THE PURVANCHAL RANGE

Moving downward and eastward from the Himalayas, we encounter the beautiful Purvanchal Range. Also known as the Eastern Highlands, this range spreads across Arunachal Pradesh, Nagaland, Mizoram, Tripura, Manipur and the eastern parts of Assam. It's been mentioned frequently in the ancient epic, the Mahabharata, which tells us how old it is. The highest point of this range stands at around 15,000 feet above sea level.

Did you know?
In Sanskrit, *purva* means 'eastern' and *achal* means 'mountain'.

Of hills and dales

There are several hills that run in a criss-cross pattern through this range, some high and some much lower. The Mizo Hills, the Naga Hills and the Mishmi Hills are some of them. At one time, these hills were ruled by the Ahoms, a dynasty that went on to rule Assam. Much later, they came under the British, like the rest of India.

Earth-shaking

This entire region is said to be very earthquake-prone. It has faults in the earth that go criss-cross across it. That is why people built lightweight houses made of bamboo, on stilts.

Working away

Because it is watered by rivers like the Lohit, Burhi Dihing, Diyung, Kusiyara and Gumti, the foothills of this range are quite fertile. Farming is an important occupation here, and rice, millet, potatoes, barley and wheat are some of the crops that grow easily in this area. People also raise poultry and other livestock. The local tribes are an industrious lot and they make some lovely handicrafts that are famous all over India.

The highest peak in these mountains is Mount Dapha, at more than 15,000 feet above sea level.

Same or different?

How many differences can you spot in these two houses typical of the Purvanchal Range?

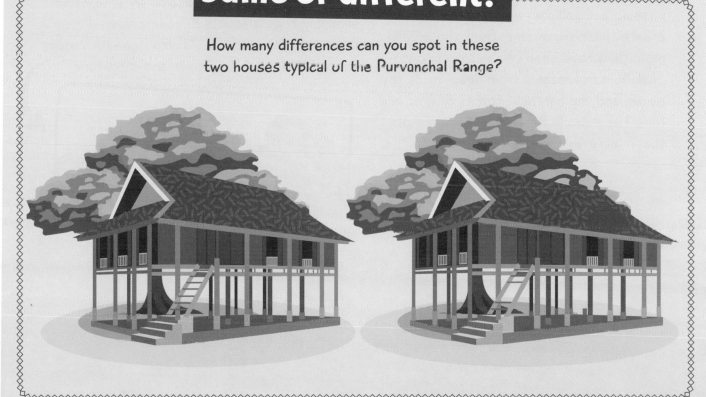

THE ARAVALLI RANGE

Moving away from the Himalayas, we travel to the Aravalli Range. This hill system goes in a slant from the north towards the south-west, like a slash. It starts near Delhi and goes through Haryana, Rajasthan and Gujarat. If you were to see the Aravalli Range from outer space, it would look like tiger tracks on a flat stretch of land. The hills are not dramatically high and range between 1000 and 3000 feet above sea level. The climate in these hills ranges from freezing in the higher reaches to moderately cool as you go lower.

Nature decides

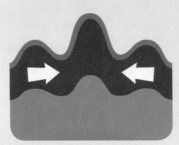

Orologists, the people who study mountains, believe that it must have taken almost two billion years of forces below the earth, shoving, pushing and colliding against each other to create these mountains. Over the millennia, mountains have seen volcanic eruptions, onslaughts of magma from deep inside the earth, and the harshest forces of wind and rain. The Aravalli Range was born out of these incredible forces of nature.

In Sanskrit, the words *ara* and *valli* mean 'a line of peaks'. And that's exactly what the Aravallis are.

Rock away

The Aravalli Range has some dense forests towards the south. But as you go north, the hills become shorter and squatter and finally disappear. The mountains effectively stop the spread of the vast desert of central India. Thanks to their geological history, the mountains are made of massive areas of stone, sand and huge amounts of rose-coloured quartzite. The land here is also rich with various minerals like marble, granite and sandstone.

River rush

Several rivers are born in the hills and valleys of the Aravallis. The Banas, the Luni, the Sakhi and the Sabarmati are some of them—the last being best known for its banks, along which Mahatma Gandhi had his ashram in Gujarat.

Wild and wonderful

Even though a large part of these mountains is rocky and barren, the parts that do have forests are lush and beautiful. The Mangar Bani forest is one such part. It is said to be home to rare plant species and animals like the jackal, nilgai and mongoose. At one time, leopards roamed this area in plenty.

Under threat

The forests and indeed the Aravallis themselves are under threat because of careless mining. People have dug deep pits into the sides of the mountains to get to the precious minerals that lie below. Sadly, this ruins trees and plants and endangers wildlife too! These activities are banned in certain places and strict action is taken against people who break these rules.

STOP

THE VINDHYA RANGE

The Vindhyas are a broken range of hills that travel from Gujarat across Madhya Pradesh and end up in Uttar Pradesh. They're regarded as a broken range because the hills are interrupted by plateaus and plains. The Malwa Plateau and the Kaimur Range are two of the better-known landforms in these hills. Amarkantak, at over 3000 feet above sea level, is the tallest peak of the Vindhya Range. Bhopal and Indore are two important cities that lie on the tableland in the heart of the Vindhyas.

Where rivers are born

Even though the mountains here are not as high as the Himalayas, they still do give rise to some important rivers. The much-revered Narmada comes crashing down the southern slopes and flows right into the Arabian Sea. While the northern slopes have some of the tributaries of Ganges, like the Kali Sindh, Parbati, Betwa and Ken. The Son, an important river for navigation, makes its presence felt towards the east.

Did you know?
The Vindhyas are known by different local names as they make their way through different regions. Some of them are Bhanrer, Kaimur and Panna.

This range, it is said, marks the traditional border between north India and south India. According to mythology, this was where the Indo-Aryan boundary ended.

Legends and tales

The Vindhyas have been mentioned several times in ancient epics like the Mahabharata. According to legend, they were full of dangerous forests with wild animals, demons and cannibals. The legends probably referred to the tribes that roamed these forests. Some believe that the goddess Shakti resided here after she slew demons. She is sometimes referred to as Vindhyavasini (dweller of the Vindhyas).

Going wild

The Vindhyas have a number of wildlife sanctuaries, especially in Madhya Pradesh. One of the most prominent ones is the Bandhavgarh National Park, which lies in the heart of the Vindhyas. It sits in a bowl that is circled by the Vindhyan cliffs and mountains. At one time, it had the highest number of tigers in the country. Sadly, this number has reduced because of poaching and hunting—both of which are now banned.

Twin tigers

Can you find twin tigers in this group? They need to be identical in every way.

THE SATPURA RANGE

The Satpura Range is a part of the Deccan Plateau. The hills make a journey of over 900 km across Maharashtra and Madhya Pradesh, crossing the massive peninsula that sits in central India. There are three smaller ranges that form the Satpuras: the Mahadeo Hills, the Maikala Hills and the Rajpipla Hills. The highest points of these hills go to almost 4000 feet above sea level.

Satpura means 'the seven folds' in Sanskrit.

The birthplace of important rivers

Some of India's most important rivers are born in the Satpuras. The Narmada originates in these hills and makes its way through the Vindhyas too. The Tapti meets the Arabian Sea in Surat. The Godavari and Mahanadi, two other important rivers, are not born here but meander through a part of the Satpuras.

Once upon a time

At one time, the Satpuras had heavily forested areas. Although it has lost a lot of its forest cover because of trees being cut for development, it still has some dense jungles. Some amazing wildlife roams amongst the trees and hills. The Bengal tiger, the barasingha, gaur, sloth bear and blackbuck are some. Some of these are critically endangered.

Natural wealth

You could say that the Satpuras have a lot of natural wealth. They are rich in minerals, in forests and wildlife. There is not too much agriculture in these hills. The few tribes that live here, like the Gonds, do grow some crops, using the *jhum* cultivation method.

Legendary

The Satpuras too have their share of myths. It is said that there is an underground city below the mountains. The legend goes that Lord Krishna shut some evil rakshasas into the city and locked the gates. Of course, this has never been proved but it certainly adds excitement to any visit to these hills.

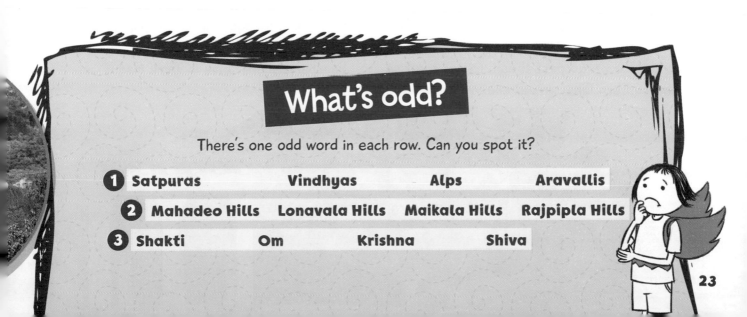

What's odd?

There's one odd word in each row. Can you spot it?

1. Satpuras   Vindhyas   Alps   Aravallis

2. Mahadeo Hills   Lonavala Hills   Maikala Hills   Rajpipla Hills

3. Shakti   Om   Krishna   Shiva

23

THE GHATS

Imagine a cheese sandwich. The Eastern and Western Ghats are like the two slices of bread and the Deccan plateau is like the cheese in between. The Western Ghats run parallel to the Arabian Sea in the west, while the Eastern Ghats run parallel to the Bay of Bengal in the east.

THE EASTERN GHATS

Did you know?

Ghat, in Sanskrit, means 'steps'. In India, most holy rivers have steps called ghats leading to the riverbank, allowing pilgrims to bathe. It also means 'mountain pass' in some Indian languages.

The Eastern Ghats are a collection of hills that make their way from the north-east to the south-west, in line with the Bay of Bengal coastline. They create a rather narrow range that journeys through the states of Odisha, Andhra Pradesh, Telangana and Tamil Nadu. A small part spills into Kerala and Karnataka too. The topography of the hills in each state is different. On average, the hills reach a height of 2000 feet above sea level. Only a few peaks reach close to 4000 feet.

Mind the gap

The hills of the Eastern Ghats are punctured or broken from time to time to make way for some important rivers. The Godavari, the Krishna, the Mahanadi and the Kaveri are some. As the hills move south, they are called the Javadi Hills and Shevaroy Hills. And once we go past these, to our surprise, the Eastern Ghats meet the Western Ghats.

Names and names

There are different hills in the various states the range traverses. Each has a different name and topography. Mahendragiri, Ramgiri and Udaygiri are some in Odisha; Galikonda, Madgol and Chintapalli are some in Andhra Pradesh; and the Bodhamalai and Panchamalai are some in Tamil Nadu.

Jungle story

There are different types of jungles and forests in the hills that make up the Eastern Ghats. Depending on their heights and their location, the forest covers on these hills varies. From evergreen forests to deciduous forests to tropical forests, these hills have them all.

Tribal tales

Scores of tribes have roamed the hills of the Eastern Ghats for generations. Though some tribes have modernized, most still lead fairly nomadic and primitive lives. Bagata, Gadaba, Jatapu, Savara, Konda Reddi and Koya are just a few. For several centuries, these tribes have been following a kind of shifting cultivation that's called podu in some areas.

Coasting along

The Eastern Ghats leave a strip of coastal plain that is called the Coromandel Coast. Because it is drained by so many rivers, it's a great spot for agriculture. It's also been called the 'land of the temples' because it has some of India's most famous temples.

So wild

There's quite a lot of wildlife that call the forests of the Eastern Ghats their home. These include tigers, leopards, sloth bears, smooth-coated otters, chital, four-horned antelopes, the ever-present bison and more. But sadly, much of their habitat is being destroyed, as people are cutting trees for agriculture, railways and plantations.

How cool! There are some national parks here where we can see some amazing wildlife. Papikonda National Park, Vedanthangal Bird Sanctuary, Kambalkona Sanctuary and Coringa Sanctuary are some that you'd love to explore.

25

THE WESTERN GHATS

The Western Ghats go in a steep slope towards the sea, along India's west coast. They reach a height of between 3000 and 5000 feet above sea level at different points. There are deep cuts and slashes in the slopes made by streams and valleys. They form a long stretch of mountains that travel through a part of Gujarat, Maharashtra, Goa, Karnataka, Kerala and Tamil Nadu. That's a long, long journey! They run along the coast, leaving a strip of coastal plains—known as the Konkan Coast. At the toe of the Western Ghats are the Nilgiris.

In Maharashtra and Gujarat, the Western Ghats are also known as the Sahyadris.

Rain, rain, come again!

The Western Ghats are considered critical for India's monsoon pattern. The rain-filled monsoon clouds that come sweeping in from the Arabian Sea are stopped in their tracks by the Western Ghats. These Ghats are said to have the world's most important tropical monsoon systems. And here's how this helps. The rains they receive, make the Western Ghats a key water source, with significant rivers being born here. It also helps sustain dense forests and along with them, a plethora of wildlife.

Rivers are born

The Godavari, the Kaveri, the Krishna and the Tungabhadra are some of the rivers that are born in the Western Ghats. Along with their tributaries, these and the other rivers make this area fertile; the conditions are perfect for trees and forests to grow. Depending on the height and location, there are several types of forests, ranging from deciduous to rainforests and even some grasslands.

A hotspot for biodiversity

Biodiversity means the number and types of animal and plant species a region has. And the forests of Western Ghats certainly have a vast and diverse collection. It is said that this range has the rarest types of trees and plants, along with some highly endangered animals and birds, and rare reptiles too! The black panther, leopard, lion-tailed macaque, monitor lizard, dwarf gecko and Malabar flying lizard are just a few. Some of these species are found only in India.

Did you know?
The Western Ghats are listed by UNESCO as a biodiversity hotspot that must be preserved forever.

Tribal tract

The hills of the Western Ghats have been home to numerous tribes. As they move through the states, the culture of the tribes changes. Invariably, the tribal people live off the land as honey gatherers, hunters, farmers and more recently, labourers. Some of the tribes living amidst these hills are the Warli, Konkana and Katkaris.

THE ANAIMALAI HILLS

These picturesque hills are also called Elephant Mountains. They are part of the Western Ghats, but have a distinct personality of their own. Most of these hills fall in the state of Tamil Nadu. From their highest point, the Anai Peak at over 8500 feet above sea level, they descend towards the sea, forming terraces along the way.

Forest fun

There are lots of dense forests in these hills. Rosewood, sandalwood, teak and sago palm trees are some of the trees that dot the slopes. Naturally, this makes for great wildlife. Gaur, elephants, tigers, panthers, sloth bears, pangolins, black-headed orioles, crocodiles, civet cats, dhole and the highly endangered lion-tailed macaques roam these forests.

Coffee or tea, anyone?

The rich soil on these slopes is terrific for growing tea and coffee. There are lush plantations here, but sadly, while planting these, much of the forest area has been cleared—causing substantial deforestation and harm to animals.

Working hard

The tribes and local people living among these hills are a busy lot. A large number of them work on tea and coffee estates. The cottage industry is well known, and residents make lovely handicraft using easily available materials like coir and metal.

Munnar moments

Munnar is one of the most famous spots in the Anamalai Hills. With a hill to its own name, Munnar is best known for its majestic tea plantations.

Time for a brew

How many cups of tea or coffee can you find in this jumble?

THE NILGIRI HILLS

The Nilgiri Hills, at the southernmost tip of the Western Ghats, are famous for their stunning landscapes. They have more than twenty-four tall peaks, the highest of which is called Doddabetta, soaring at a height of 8500 feet above sea level. Hundreds of people trudge up to see the spectacular views. These hills are much wetter and colder than the plains that surround them.

How can a mountain be blue?

Nilgiri literally means 'blue mountain'. Some say the mountains earned the name because of a beautiful blue flower called the Strobilanthes—better known as *neelakurunji*—which grows wild in the forests. Some others believe that it is because when you see the Nilgiri mountains from far, they look blue.

Mmmmm, what's that lovely smell?

The fragrant eucalyptus tree grows in plenty in the Nilgiri area. If you walk through the forests, you can't help but smell its fragrance. People make oil from this tree as it is said to be highly medicinal. The hills are also perfect for growing tea, coffee and various vegetables. There are some massive tea estates that are spread across these valleys.

A British feel

Just like in the Himalayas, here too the British kept seeking places where they would get the same cold, wet climate from back home. They built towns in the upper reaches of the Nilgiris. Udhagamandalam (popularly known as Ooty) and Coonoor are two such towns.

Staying home

The original residents of the Nilgiri Hills were the tribes called Toda, Badaga, Kota, Irula and Kurumbas. Most of these tribes still live here, but now some of them are occupied in jobs on tea estates and other more modern activities like tourism.

Mountain maze

Can you trace a path by following the mountains of India along this maze?

Himalayas	Alps	Rockies	Andes	Balkan	Blue Ridge	Jungfrau
Siwalik	Karakoram	Pir Panjal	Hindu Kush	Teton	Jura	Matterhorn
Ural	Pyrenees	Zanskar	Dolomites	Titlis	Gangdise	Eiger
Appalachian	Tian Shan	Purvanchal	Aravalli	Tatra	Palatine	Monch
Atlas	Altai Zagros	Alborz	Vindhya	Satpura	Eastern Ghats	Säntis
Caucasus	Alaska	Antarctica	Lone	Pilander	Western Ghats	Anaimalai
Rehberg	Cypress	Gorgaburu	Pizol	Pica	Langkofel	Nilgiris

RIVERS

Since the beginning of time, humans and animals have made their homes near rivers and other waterbodies. Naturally! Water, apart from air, is the most important element we need to survive. The world's greatest cities are built around rivers. London has the Thames, Rome has the Tiber, Paris has the Seine and Vienna has the Danube. And India? India has hundreds of rivers—both large and small—that go around the vast country, watering it, feeding the crops and sustaining its over billion people. That's a lot of tasks for any river to do!

Holier than holy

In India, people have recognized the importance of rivers to such an extent that rivers are considered gods, and people pray to them! Some rivers even have personalities and proper deities. There are numerous legends associated with them. And invariably, there are scores of temples—big and small—on riverbanks.

Did you know?
Most of India's rivers are female, barring a few. That's not all! Girls are named for rivers, like Ganga, Yamuna, Kaveri and Godavari.

So why are rivers so important?

1   They help farmers by watering fields.
2   They provide drinking water to us and to plants and animals.
3   They help us generate electricity through the dams we build on them. And where would we be without power!
4   They help carry goods and equipment up and down their streams.
5   There is precious wildlife and fish that live in them.
6   They help plants, trees and the environment in a hundred different ways.

Rivers of India

We know that India is an enormous country. And if the mountains are like the bones of India, the rivers function like the arteries and veins, criss-crossing busily across the land. There are two kinds of main rivers in India.

- The Himalayan rivers: These are created by melting snows and glaciers, and so these flow right through the year.

- The peninsular rivers: These are born in India's peninsula and flow either east into the Bay of Bengal, or west into the Arabian Sea. Many are fed by rains and can run dry during a bad monsoon.

River alert

Unfortunately, Indian rivers are being carelessly polluted. Also, owing to the unplanned dams being built on them, the waters of some rivers are being diverted and there is considerable environmental damage. The environmentalists and other organizations are doing all they can to clean and protect our rivers, which do so much for us.

Oh wow! Typically, rivers in India are referred to as Mother. For example, people say Ganga Ma or Saraswati Ma. That's because they know that rivers give them so much, just like a mother does.

THE CHENAB

Let's start right at the very top, with the Chenab. This is India's northernmost river, born in the Himalayas in Himachal Pradesh. There are two rivers called Chandra and Bhaga, which come together here to form the Chenab. This mighty river cuts deep valleys and gorges and flows through Jammu and Kashmir before making its way into Pakistan. It also joins the Sutlej, another important river that India shares with Pakistan. It flows for almost a thousand kilometres.

Oh wow! The Indian Railways is building the highest railway bridge in the world across the Chenab. Its soaring arch is a sight to behold!

Melting snow

During summer, when the snow melts, the Chenab is in full flow. There are several dams and hydroelectric projects on this river because of the force of the water as it thunders down from the mountaintops.

What's in a name?

Mentioned in the Mahabharata as Chandrabhaga, the Chenab has been around for a long time. Historians have even found references of it in ancient Greek manuscripts, under the name Sandrophagos, Sandabaga and Cantabra. Alexander the Great built towns near this river when he invaded India through the Himalayas. It was probably the influence of the Persian language that finally gave it its current name—Chenab.

Crack the code

One of the Chenab's names is hidden in this puzzle. Crack the code to find it.

A=1 N=2 C=3 T=6 R=4 B=9

3	1	2	6	1	9	4	1

THE SUTLEJ

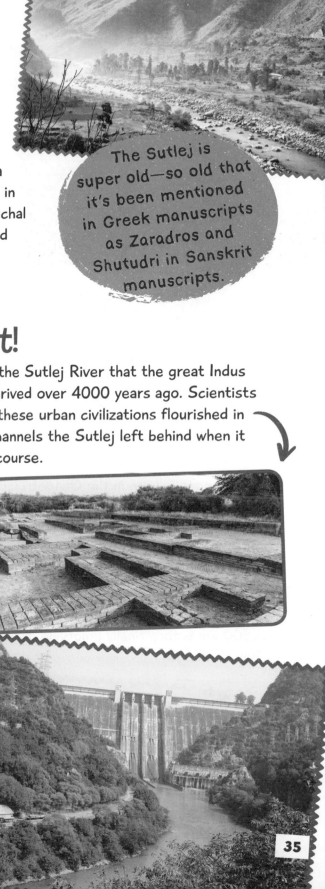

The Sutlej is the longest of Punjab's five rivers and flows for 1400 km across mountains and plains. It is a tributary of the massive Indus River, which gave India its name and now flows in Pakistan. Although it is born in the Himalayan region of Tibet, the Sutlej crosses Himachal Pradesh before entering Punjab to join the Chenab, and finally spills into Pakistan.

The Sutlej is super old—so old that it's been mentioned in Greek manuscripts as Zaradros and Shutudri in Sanskrit manuscripts.

The Tibetan connection

A part of the Sutlej valley that lay in Tibet was called the Garuda Valley by the Zhangzhung civilization that lived there. Remnants of their monuments are still found there. Now, several centuries later, the Sutlej valley has tribal descendants of the Zhangzhung, some of whom breed sheep and yaks.

The power of the Sutlej

The power and force with which the Sutlej comes crashing down the mountainsides, makes it perfect for setting up hydroelectric plants. Almost half of the power that the state of Himachal Pradesh uses is generated by the Sutlej!

Oh-so ancient!

It was along the Sutlej River that the great Indus civilization thrived over 4000 years ago. Scientists believe that these urban civilizations flourished in the empty channels the Sutlej left behind when it changed its course.

The famous Bhakra Nangal Dam is on the Sutlej River.

THE GANGES

How can we ever talk about India's rivers without talking about the Ganges? The Ganges—or Ganga, as it is better known in Indian languages—is by far India's most religious and important river. Not only because it has loads of tributaries creating an incredibly fertile basin but also because it is worshipped as a goddess by millions. Let's dive into the story of the Ganges.

Did you know?
The river Ganges, when depicted as a goddess, has over 100 names?

Where the Ganges is born

The Ganges is born in the Gangotri Glacier, high up in the Himalayas. The Gaumukh (meaning 'mouth of a cow') is a glacier cave, and it is said to be the very spot that the Ganges begins. Millions of pilgrims visit it to pray to the Ganges. The river comes crashing down about 14,000 feet down steep valleys and cliffs. It travels more than 2500 km before finally emptying itself into the Bay of Bengal.

Tributaries and offshoots

The Ganges, along with its tributaries, waters the massive Indo-Gangetic Plain, making the region fertile and perfect for farmers to grow crops. The Bhagirathi, the Alaknanda, the Mandakini, the Dhauliganga and the Pindar are some of its tributaries that rise in the mountains of Uttarakhand. As the Ganges flows down, the amount of water increases with more rivers joining it. During summer, melting snow fills it with more water than it can sometimes handle, resulting in floods.

More than a river

For Hindus, the Ganga is literally a goddess. In mythology, the river is depicted as a lovely lady dressed in white, often riding a *makara* (a sort of a crocodile), or sitting or standing on a lotus, or even riding a dolphin. According to the Mahabharata, Ganga was the mother of Bhishma, the beloved uncle of the warring cousins, the Pandavas and Kauravas. People believe that the Ganga is so pure that its water helps people get rid of their sins. Millions go to the banks of the great river to take a dip, believing that this will purify them.

The water of the Ganges is called Gangajal. Devout Hindus keep a bottle of it handy, and when a person is ill or about to pass away, they are fed the water, with the belief that all their sins will be washed away.

Which one is different?

One of these images of the goddess Ganga is different.
Can you spot it?

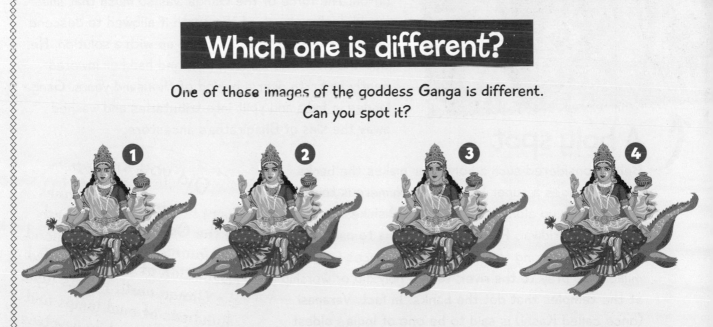

1   2   3   4

Legends galore

There are legends aplenty about how the Ganges came to be. One myth says that Lord Vishnu pierced a hole in the universe with his toe, to allow the Ganges to flow over his feet and down to Earth. Because the river touched Lord Vishnu's feet, it is also known as Vishnupadi, meaning 'one who descended from Vishnu's feet'.

The hair of Shiva

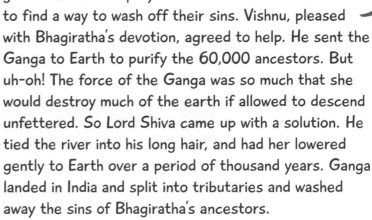

Yet another myth goes thus. The mythological king Bhagiratha discovered that 60,000 of his ancestors had sinned and couldn't get to heaven. He prayed to Vishnu to find a way to wash off their sins. Vishnu, pleased with Bhagiratha's devotion, agreed to help. He sent the Ganga to Earth to purify the 60,000 ancestors. But uh-oh! The force of the Ganga was so much that she would destroy much of the earth if allowed to descend unfettered. So Lord Shiva came up with a solution. He tied the river into his long hair, and had her lowered gently to Earth over a period of thousand years. Ganga landed in India and split into tributaries and washed away the sins of Bhagiratha's ancestors.

A holy spot

Being considered such a holy river makes the banks of the Ganges a super busy place. Numerous towns have sprung up along its banks, like Rishikesh, Varanasi, Haridwar, Prayagraj and Patna to name a few. People throng to these religious places by the millions to pray to the river, take a holy dip or worship at the temples that dot the banks. In fact, Varanasi (once called Kashi) is said to be one of India's oldest cities and is mentioned in ancient scriptures. Scores of mystics, sadhus and monks wander these cities.

Did you know?

Every evening, on the banks of the Ganges in Rishikesh and Varanasi, there is a grand celebration of the river, called the Ganga aarti. Priests light hundreds of mud lamps and sing a bhajan while devotees pray fervently.

As seen from outer space

The Kumbh Mela, one of the world's largest human congregations, takes place here. It's held once every twelve years somewhere on the banks of the Ganges or its principal tributaries. The collection of people is so large that it can even be seen from outer space.

In the wild

Although the Ganges is most known for its holy water, it also plays host to a large number of wildlife species. It is believed to be one of the world's most biodiverse river systems. It has around 140 species of fish, ninety species of amphibians and more than 300 bird species swimming, flying, creeping and crawling in the waters and the banks. One of the most famous is the Gangetic dolphin, found in very few places in the world. The Sundarbans mangroves that are created by the tributaries of the Ganges have the world's last surviving mangrove tigers.

Watch out!

Here's something ironic. Though people believe that the water of the Ganges purifies them, it is said to be among the world's most polluted rivers. Human waste, industrial waste and pesticides—it has it all. This kind of pollution not only threatens wildlife but also causes diseases in people. Governments and voluntary organizations are trying hard to control the pollution and make the Ganges what it is, when it first starts its journey from the Himalayan glaciers—pure and clean.

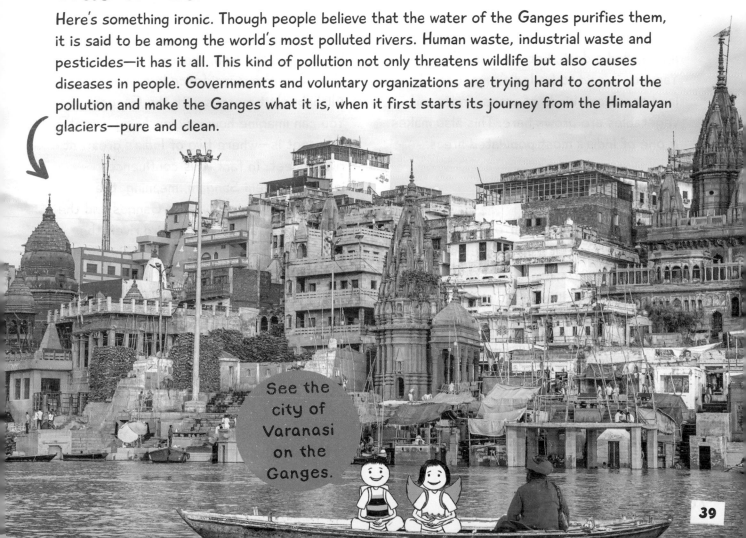

See the city of Varanasi on the Ganges.

THE YAMUNA

We now come to another sacred river. The Yamuna (known as Jamuna in some parts) rises in the Himalayan glaciers. Its birthplace is called Yamunotri. It comes crashing down steep mountainsides and makes its way through the states of Uttarakhand and Uttar Pradesh over a distance of over 1300 km. It's probably the most well-known tributary of the Ganges.

A hard-working river

Although the Yamuna allows only light traffic to pass on it, it does a great job at irrigating the lands it passes through. An area called a doab, between the Ganges and Yamuna, is said to be India's most fertile land as various kinds of crops, fruits and vegetables are grown here. This also makes it one of India's most populated areas.

Busy towns

There are a large number of important and lively towns located on the banks of the Yamuna. Delhi, Agra, Prayagraj, Mathura, Noida and Etawah are some.

Tributary cousins

As the Yamuna makes its way across the land, it is joined by some important tributaries like the Chambal, the Sindh, the Betwa, the Ken, the Tons and the Giri. Near Prayagraj (once known as Allahabad), it merges with the Ganges. You can imagine how religiously important this spot is—where two of India's greatest rivers meet. In fact, this confluence is called Triveni Sangam, meaning 'the meeting of the trinity'. The Ganges and the Yamuna are said to join a third river, the mythological Saraswati River, at this point. Now one with the Ganges, the two rivers together go on to meet the Bay of Bengal.

Oh wow! The world-famous Taj Mahal sits on one of the banks of the Yamuna.

Lore and legends

The Yamuna too has its share of legends. Yami and Yama were the twin children of the sun god Surya. When Yama died, Yami was so grief-stricken that she wept for days, her tears flooding the land and eventually turning into the Yamuna River. Yet another legend is about Lord Krishna, who lived in Mathura by the banks of the Yamuna. One day, a fierce serpent monster called Kaliya took over the river and poisoned it. People and animals could no longer drink its water. Krishna, who was just a young lad, took matters into his own hands. He lured the serpent out and danced on its head till it fell dead.

Did you know?
In some temples, Yamuna is shown as a goddess, riding a tortoise. It is said that the riverbank has tortoises crawling around.

Pollution, pollution everywhere!

More than 50 million people live off the Yamuna. Tragically, the waters of this famous river are heavily polluted, with industrial and human waste. The waste also collects because for a large part of the year, the river is stagnant. There are movements being carried out to clean up the Yamuna.

THE TRIBUTARIES OF THE GANGES

You're probably wondering how many tributaries the Ganges has. The answer is: lots! Some are major rivers in their own right, and several have smaller tributaries of their own too.

THE GHAGHARA

THE GANDAK

This tributary of the Ganges makes its appearance as the Karnali River high up in the Tibetan Himalayas. It comes through Nepal into India, journeying through the states of Uttar Pradesh and Bihar. It thunders through the Siwalik range and finally meets its elder sibling, the Ganges, in a place called Chapra in Bihar. Together with its tributaries, the Kuwana, the Rapti and the Little Gandak, the Ghaghara helps the Ganges make the region very rich in fertile soils. It travels almost 1000 km before the journey's end.

Also known as the Narayani, this is yet another important tributary of the Ganges. The Gandak is born in the Himalayas in Nepal. It flows south into India, cutting deep valleys along the way. It travels along the border of Uttar Pradesh and Bihar and after a journey of over 750 km, it finally meets the Ganges somewhere near the city of Patna. Apart from helping the Ganges water the incredibly fertile Indo-Gangetic Plain, the Gandak also hosts some forests with terrific wildlife.

Did you know?
The Ghaghara turns into the Sarju River as it goes south. The second-century geographer, Ptolemy, mentioned it as the Sarabos all those years ago.

THE GOMTI

The Gomati, or Gumti (as it is sometimes known), rises in Uttar Pradesh. It travels for more than 900 km through the state, before meeting up with the Ganges. This river, according to mythology, is the daughter of Sage Vashishtha. The Mahabharata was first narrated along its banks, as per some legends. It's been mentioned in both the ancient epics, Ramayana and Mahabharata. There are a number of temples dedicated to various deities along its banks. Lucknow is the most important town that depends on the Gomti water.

THE KOSI

The Kosi River (or Koshi as it is sometimes called) flows mainly in Nepal and Tibet, but also makes its way into India through the Siwalik range. It emerges in India and enters Bihar on its way to meeting the Ganges. It makes a journey of over 700 km. It's dreaded for its frequent floods because of its force and power. The good thing is that this power is also harnessed for electricity.

Legends say the god of death took a woman's form and began to live on the banks of the Kosi. In ancient sculptures, this goddess is depicted as a carefree woman, or as a fierce destroyer. Sometimes her waters help farms to grow and sometimes destroy them with fierce floods.

Make the match

Match the river to its legend.

Kosi

Ganga

Yamuna

Gomti

Twin sister of Yama

Daughter of Sage Vashishtha

The god of death

Descended from Lord Shiva's hair

THE BRAHMAPUTRA

The majestic Brahmaputra is one of India's most powerful rivers. It is known by different names in the various countries it meanders through—the Tsangpo in Tibet, the Yarlung Zangbo Jiang in China, and Jamuna (not to be mixed up with India's Yamuna) in Bangladesh. It's born in the Himalayas and travels about 1800 miles. It enters India through Arunachal Pradesh, where it is called the Siang or Diang. It then travels through Assam before completing its final journey along with the Ganges—where the mixed waters of both rivers pour into the Bay of Bengal.

At last! The Brahmaputra is one of the few 'male' rivers in India. The name means the 'son of Brahma, the creator of the universe'.

Oh wow! The old Sanskrit name for the Brahmaputra is Lauhitya, meaning 'red like blood'. Some say that the name is the Sanskritized version of *bullam buthur*, which in the tribal Bodo language mean 'a gurgling sound'.

Power play

The power of the Brahmaputra is awe-inspiring. It is said to be the youngest of the important world river systems, but it's no less powerful. Although in its higher reaches, it's not navigable because of fierce currents, as it enters the plains it is used for transport and carrying goods. But watch out for its force. It's known as both a creator and a destroyer. Though it brings with it fertile soil, which is great for farmers, it also tends to cause floods and destruction.

A moving ocean

The river is so massive and wide that it is known as a 'moving ocean' in Assam. At its widest, it is over 16 km wide, and when you're in the middle, you cannot see either bank. Its river basin is so massive that it covers four countries: Bhutan, India, Tibet and Bangladesh. Its banks see a lot of erosion, which means the soil becomes loose because of the force of the water. It is dangerous to build permanent structures along such areas.

One of the reasons the Brahmaputra is so powerful is that it is fed by nearly thirty tributaries along its journey.

Towns and bridges

There are both large and small towns along the banks of the Brahmaputra. The largest of these is Guwahati. This large city was once the capital of the Kamarupa Hindu kingdom. It later changed hands and went to the Ahoms, who ruled Assam for years. There are also several bridges that are built across this mighty river. The Bogibeel Bridge in Assam is almost 5 km long and stretches across the river. Built as a rail-cum-road bridge, the railway tracks on this bridge are among India's longest.

Bridge it!

You need to use lots of bridges to cross this river. Solve this maze and reach home soon.

A treasure of wildlife

The waters of the Brahmaputra are home to a vast number of river creatures. The wetlands that the massive river creates along with its tributaries is called a beel and is known as an ecotonal zone, which indicates that it is great for ecology and biodiversity. The forests and grasslands along this mighty river have scores of wild beasts—right from tigers to clouded leopards, barasingha, sloth bears and wild water buffaloes to name just a few.

Awesome! The one-horned rhinoceros, which is found only in Assam, is also a resident of the floodplains of the Brahmaputra.

Tribal tract

There are a number of tribes that make their living off the Brahmaputra. The Mishing (the largest), the Deori, the Sonowal Kachari and the Adi are some that live right by the river. Cultivating crops is their main occupation, but the frequent flooding makes their lives hard.

Legends and lore

Like with some other rivers in India, the Brahmaputra too has its share of legends and myths associated with it. Some may seem like fantasy, though the local people not just believe them but also derive strength from them.

How the river became red

One legend tells the story of how the river became *lohit* or red, giving it the name Lohitya. A son, born to Lord Brahma, took the form of water. He grew into a great lake called the Brahmakunda. Now it so happened that Parashurama, an incarnation of Lord Vishnu, had committed the heinous crime of murder. During the scuffle leading to the murder, an axe got stuck in his arm. Parashurama was advised to take a dip in the Brahmakunda to wash off his sin. As soon as he did so, the axe fell off, leaving the water blood red. And this, some believe, is what made the river red.

Crossword time

Mishki and Pushka know quite a lot about rivers by now.
Can you help them solve this crossword?

DOWN

1 Where India's most important river is born
2 Another name for the Gandak
4 The river that has a twin brother according to legend
5 India's most important river
7 Lucknow is this river's most important town

ACROSS

3 The Chenab is known by this name in the epics
6 The rhino, living along the Brahmaputra, is a resident of this state
8 This bridge on the Brahmaputra has two tiers

THE HOOGHLY

The Hooghly River has always been crucial to India's trade. It is formed by the coming together of the Bhagirathi and Jalangi rivers in the state of West Bengal. It's an arm of the Ganges and flows for about 260 km before it joins the Bay of Bengal. As it nears its end, it is fed by other smaller rivers, creating a wide estuary. Two of its main tributaries are the Damodar and the Rupnarayan rivers.

Ever so busy

The route that the Hooghly takes is a very busy one. There are towns and industries around it—the main one being the cities of Kolkata and Howrah. In fact, it's one of the few rivers that allows ocean-going ships to sail on it, all the way into Kolkata.

A centre of trade

Historically, the Hooghly has always been a waterway for traders. Centuries ago, the East India Company made Kolkata (then called Calcutta) their capital because it was their main trading centre. Even the Portuguese, Dutch and French traders built trade settlements along the banks of the Hooghly. For years, Kolkata has been one of India's busiest river ports. Haldia is now the main port on the Hooghly.

Oh-so diverse!

There are parts of the Hooghly that are surrounded only by sandbanks and mud formations, especially as it approaches the Bay of Bengal. But a little further north, it is surrounded by green fields of rice and paddy, quaint villages and beautiful groves.

The wonder bridge

The Howrah Bridge is probably one of Bengal's most famous monuments. It is an engineering marvel that the British built across the river Hooghly. It took seven years to build, which seems pretty quick. It is one of the busiest bridges in the world, with lakhs of people and cars crossing over it every day. Wow!

During the various periods that European traders settled in this area, they built some lovely mansions and buildings. A few of these still exist along the banks of the Hooghly. Sadly, most are in ruins, though some have been restored.

Puzzled!

Mishki and Pushka are puzzled because they can't figure out what this hidden word is. Can you help them?
Hint: It's the tributary of a famous river.

A N P R U A Y N R A

THE NARMADA

The Narmada, a river that flows mainly through central India, is an important route between the Ganges river valley and the Arabian Sea. One of India's most beautiful rivers, the Narmada is born in the Maikal Range in Madhya Pradesh. It is also known as Nerbudda or Narbada. The ancient Greek geographer, Ptolemy, referred to it as Namade in his writings.

A winding course

Having been born at a height of more than 3500 feet, the Narmada comes thundering down and carves a winding route through the hills. It slices through the Vindhya and Satpura ranges, creating some dramatic waterfalls along the way. It then finds its way westward into the state of Gujarat. It ends its 1300-km-long journey in the Gulf of Khambat in the Arabian Sea.

A sacred river

Hindus regard the Narmada as a sacred river, almost a mother, and probably second only to the Ganges in how holy it is. The people living in its valleys and fertile basins believe that a dip in the Narmada will not only wash off sins but also stop the cycle of birth and death for them. They perform a highly religious journey called the parikrama—which involves them walking along the entire length of the river—on both banks. It's said that this journey takes people at least three-and-a-half years of walking continuously to complete this journey.

The daughter of Shiva

According to a popular legend, Lord Shiva performed the dance of destruction when his beloved wife Kali died. People believe that the sweat poured off him and turned into the river Narmada.

In the eye of a storm

During the last several years, the Narmada has been at the centre of much argument and discussion. For centuries, the Narmada valley has sheltered and grown hundreds of villages. In order to generate more hydroelectric power and increase irrigation, the government proposed the building of dams, the main one being the Sardar Sarovar Dam. This would make it the world's largest river valley development project. However, as environmentalists have pointed out, building these dams will alter the course of the river and cause a lot of destruction to villages. There were protests, and though the work on some dams was stopped, the issue is still not resolved.

The devout believe that the river Ganga comes to the Narmada once a year in the shape of a black cow. After taking a dip in the holy river, it emerges pure white.

That's odd!

There's one odd word in each row. Can you find it?

1. **Gomti**   **Ganges**   **Nile**   **Brahmaputra**

2. **Chandigarh**   **Lucknow**   **Rishikesh**   **Agra**

3. **Chenab**   **Narmada**   **Yamuna**   **Gandak**

THE MAHANADI

The name Mahanadi literally means 'great river'! This river rises in the hills of Chhattisgarh in central India. It then makes its way eastward, entering the state of Odisha. It travels more than 900 km through the forest-filled Eastern Ghats. It finally empties its waters into the Bay of Bengal through smaller channels and streams.

Fit and fertile ↗

The Mahanadi Valley is said to have very fertile soil. Agriculture flourishes here and crops like kharif and rabi are cultivated on a massive scale. Evidently, farming is a major occupation here and this entire region is dotted with small and large farms.

A dam that helps

The Hirakud Dam, built on the Mahanadi, is India's longest earthen dam. It makes water available to vast tracts of land. It also supplies massive amounts of hydroelectric power to the state of Odisha. Wait, there's more! It also helps control floods during times when the Mahanadi is overflowing, making it safe for the nearby areas.

Here's a fun fact. It is believed that some of the world's most precious diamonds were found right below the spot where the Hirakud Dam was built. In fact, *hira* means 'diamond'.

Pray away

The cities of Sambalpur and Cuttack, still very prominent, were important trading hubs in ancient times. The town of Puri, at one of the mouths of the river, is a very famous and religious spot, where millions come to pray at the twelfth century CE temple of Jagannath. There are other temples along the bank of the Mahanadi too. The Lakshmana temple, at a place called Sirpur, is believed to be over 1500 years old. The Leaning Temple of Huma, a temple dedicated to Lord Shiva, is one of the few leaning temples in the world.

Several towns have sprung up in places where temples have been built along riverbanks.

What's different?

Can you find six differences between these two pictures of a dam on a river?

THE GODAVARI

The Godavari is one of India's longest rivers. It is born in Trimbakeshwar, in the Nashik district of Maharashtra. It is almost 1500 km. It travels through Maharashtra, Telangana, Andhra Pradesh, Chhattisgarh and Odisha and finally pours into the Bay of Bengal through two mouths, the Gautami Godavari and the Vasishta Godavari. At its start, the course of the Godavari is gentle. But when it enters the Eastern Ghats, it slices through the hills, creating sharp valleys and gorges.

Tribute to tributaries

The Godavari has a massive network of tributaries. The Darna, the Purna, the Manjara, the Pranhita and the Indravati are some. Together with these, the Godavari creates a highly fertile region in the plains that it flows through. The basin of the Wainganga, one of its tributaries, is rich in wildlife.

Did you know?
There is a world-famous Shiva temple in Trimbakeshwar. A sacred pond in the heart of the temple is where people say the actual source of the Godavari is.

Dandakaranya, the forest where Lord Rama went during his exile, is said to be close to the Godavari in the Nashik region.

Town polish

There are some important religious and industrial towns along the banks of the Godavari. Nashik, Nanded, Nizamabad, Dharmapuri and Rajahmundry are a few. These are important industrial districts with factories built in and around them.

Wild and wonderful

The Godavari river delta is home to the Coringa mangrove forests as well as some thick deciduous forests. The Coringa Wildlife Sanctuary in Andhra Pradesh is well known for the numerous species of crustaceans, fish and reptiles, like the endangered olive ridley turtle.

Mystical myths

The land where the Godavari was born was once a small village. A sage called Gautama lived here. He had a gift by which anything he sowed would grow into plush fields. One day, he committed the unforgivable sin of killing a cow, sacred to Hindus. To atone for this sin, he went to Trimbakeshwar and prayed hard. Forgiving him, Lord Shiva allowed a stream of water to flow from his hair and wash off the sins of Gautama. The stream followed Gautama wherever he walked, and thus was born the Godavari.

THE KRISHNA

The Krishna River (also known as Kistna) flows in the southern and central parts of India and is among India's longer rivers. It rises amongst the hills of the Western Ghats in Maharashtra. It then travels over 1200 km across the breadth of India. It cuts through the Eastern Ghats and finally meets the Bay of Bengal. It crosses the states of Maharashtra, Karnataka, Telangana and Andhra Pradesh.

Fed by rain

The seasonal monsoon rain fills up the Krishna. So although it creates a very fertile valley, which is wonderful for growing crops, farmers can't entirely depend on the water from the river because a poor monsoon means parts of the river can run dry.

Merry cousins

Two of its largest tributaries—like its close cousins—are the Bhima in the north and the Tungabhadra in the south. There are some important hydroelectric power plants along these rivers that provide electricity to the states of Telangana and Andhra Pradesh.

Creatures of the wild

There are some magnificent forest regions along the Krishna river basin with terrific wildlife. The Bhadra Wildlife Sanctuary, Nagarjuna-Srisailam Tiger Reserve, the Koyna Wildlife Sanctuary and the Great Indian Bustard Sanctuary are some of the major sanctuaries where a lot of wonderful and rare creatures roam safely.

Cityscape

Some major cities have grown along the Krishna over the decades. Two of the most important are Sangli in Maharashtra (known as the turmeric city) and Vijayawada in Andhra Pradesh.

Blocky puzzle

Can you help Pushka fill in the blocks of this puzzle and find the hidden word in the purple square? The word is a natural element that rivers need to keep them flowing.

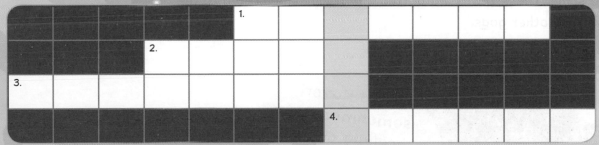

1. The name of the mangrove forests that sit in the delta of a famous river.

2. This one's a tributary of the Krishna River.

3. This river is sometimes known as the Gautami.

4. The district in which a famous river is born, and one that has a famous forest to which Lord Rama was exiled.

THE KAVERI

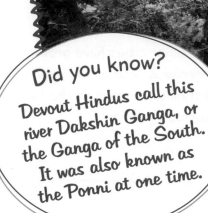

The Kaveri (sometimes spelt as Cauvery) is the most sacred river in south India. It makes an appearance in the Brahmagiri Hills in the Kodagu (once called Coorg) region of the Western Ghats in Karnataka. It plunges south through Karnataka and Tamil Nadu and then in the Eastern Ghats, it crashes down in a series of dramatic waterfalls. It makes its way to the Bay of Bengal where it finally completes its journey. Just before it empties itself into the Bay of Bengal, the Kaveri forms a wide and beautiful delta that's fondly called the 'garden of south India'.

Tributaries and towns

Several smaller rivers join the Kaveri as it makes its way to the Bay of Bengal. Some of its larger tributaries include the Harangi, Hemavati, Kabini, Bhavani and Suvarnavathi. Major towns have developed along this river. Tiruchirappalli (fondly called Trichy), Thanjavur and Srirangapatna are some. These towns are dotted with temples dedicated to the river and other gods.

Did you know?
Devout Hindus call this river Dakshin Ganga, or the Ganga of the South. It was also known as the Ponni at one time.

The Kaveri sometimes flows calmly and at other times comes gushing down hillsides with great force.

At the source

A temple town called Talacauvery (meaning 'the base of the Kaveri') in Kodagu is a famous spot for pilgrims who visit it in thousands to pray to their beloved river. This is also the very spot where the river is said to originate. So you can imagine how important it is. People believe that taking a dip in this river cures one of various ailments.

Kaveri's story

The Kaveri River is worshipped as a goddess in Karnataka and Tamil Nadu. The legend goes thus. The well-known Sage Agastya saw a beautiful maiden, Kaveri, meditating on the Brahmagiri Hills. Kaveri was the daughter of Lord Brahma and had a deep desire to serve people. Agastya fell in love with her and at once asked her to marry him. Kaveri agreed on one condition: that he would never leave her for a prolonged period. Now, as is the wont of sages, Agastya got caught up in a philosophical discussion and forgot all about his wife. Not forgetting her promise, Kaveri turned into a river and flowed away from her husband to fulfil her deepest desire—serving people.

Oh wow! The Kodavas, the tribal community that lives in Kodagu, call the river Kaveriamma, or Mother Kaveri.

THE PERIYAR

We're now down south to the southernmost large river, the Periyar. This almost 225-km-long river is born in the Western Ghats in Kerala, close to the Tamil Nadu border. Compare this to the length of the Ganges and you realize what a small river this is. But that doesn't make it any less important—especially for the people who live around it. It flows a small distance and finishes its short journey at the Periyar Lake—a lake that was created when a dam was built on it decades ago.

The Periyar is called the lifeline of Kerala—that's how important it is for the people living there.

An important job

The Periyar (meaning 'big river') is one of the few rivers in the region that is always full—which means it is perennial. It is the main source of drinking water for the towns in Kerala. That's not all—it has several hydroelectric dams that supply a large part of Kerala's electricity. And it also has a lot of fisheries, fish being one of Kerala's staple foods.

A national park

Close to Lake Periyar, around the banks of the river is a wonderful wildlife sanctuary called the Periyar National Park and Tiger Reserve. Thanks to the permanent water supply, a wide variety of animals make their home here. The gaur, a variety of deer, elephants, tigers, the lion-tailed macaque, Nilgiri langur are just some of the creatures that roam the protected area.

Pollution, pollution everywhere

Here's a sorry fact. Because the Periyar provides such abundant water, it's the perfect place for building factories that need water. The banks of the river have heavy industries built near them, and this is creating a lot of industrial pollution in the rivers. Traditional occupations like fishing and farming around the river are slowly disappearing. This is bad for the environment. Efforts are underway to make this problem disappear.

Oh wow!
That was a thrilling ride. Now to look after these amazing mountains and rivers so that they remain as wonderful for ever and ever!

River Grid

Can you find ten Indian rivers hidden in this grid?

A	S	D	F	G	H	T	H	J	U	S	A
H	G	A	N	G	F	S	H	G	J	U	K
O	Q	W	A	W	E	R	T	O	N	T	A
O	P	E	R	I	Y	A	R	M	M	L	V
G	W	T	M	S	D	F	H	T	B	E	E
H	S	Y	A	W	B	G	J	I	M	J	R
L	C	T	D	C	H	E	N	A	B	W	I
Y	V	G	A	Y	A	M	U	N	A	H	S
A	B	B	A	S	D	F	G	H	J	K	L
B	R	A	H	M	A	P	U	T	R	A	F

ANSWERS

page 7 Jumbled up
1. Rivers   2. Rain   3. Forests

page 11 Hidden countries

Q	W	E	R	T	Y	U	I	O	P
P	A	K	I	S	T	A	N	X	B
A	S	D	F	G	I	S	E	D	H
Z	X	C	V	B	B	V	B	R	U
E	D	C	R	F	Y	E	E	R	T
D	C	F	V	G	T	E	D	R	A
U	N	E	P	A	L	F	E	H	N
Z	X	S	D	C	V	F	G	B	H
R	T	Y	U	I	N	D	I	A

page 17 Same or different?

page 21 Twin tigers
I and J are identical.

page 23 What's odd?
1. Alps   2. Lonavala Hills   3. Om

page 29 Time for a brew
If you have found at least
twenty-five cups, you are a star!

page 31 Mountain maze

Himalayas	Alps	Rockies	Andes	Balkan	Blue Ridge	Jungfrau
Siwalik	Karakoram	Pir Panjal	Hindu Kush	Teton	Jura	Matterhorn
Ural	Pyrenees	Zanskar	Dolomites	Titlis	Gangdise	Eiger
Appalachian	Tian Shan	Purvanchal	Aravalli	Tetra	Palatine	Monch
Atlas	Altai Zagros	Alborz	Vindhya	Satpura	Eastern Ghats	Säntis
Caucasus	Alaska	Antarctica	Lone	Pilander	Western Ghats	Anaimalai
Rehberg	Cypress	Gorgaburu	Pizol	Pica	Langkofel	Nilgiris

page 34 Crack the code
CANTABRA

page 37 Which one is different?
The third one.

page 43 Make the match
Ganga - Descended from Lord Shiva's hair

Yamuna - Twin sister of Yama

Gomti - Daughter of Sage Vashishtha

Kosi - The god of death

page 45 Bridge it!

page 47 Crossword time

			¹G							²N	
³C	H	A	N	D	R	A	B	H	A	G	A
			G							R	
				⁴Y		⁵G				A	
				A		A				Y	
	T			M		N				A	
	R			U		G		⁷G		N	
	I			N		E		O		I	
			⁶A	S	S	A	M				
							T				
				⁸B	O	G	I	B	E	E	L

page 49 Puzzled!
RUPNARAYAN

page 51 That's odd!
1. Nile   2. Chandigarh   3. Narmada

page 53 What's different?

page 57 Blocky puzzle
1. CORINGA
2. BHIMA
3. GODAVARI
4. NASHIK

Purple blocks: RAIN

page 61 River grid

A	S	D	F	G	H	T	H	J	U	S	A
H	G	A	N	G	E	S	H	G	J	U	K
O	Q	W	A	W	E	R	T	O	N	T	A
O	P	E	R	I	Y	A	R	M	M	L	V
G	W	T	M	S	D	F	H	T	B	E	E
H	S	Y	A	W	B	G	J	I	M	J	R
L	C	T	D	C	H	E	N	A	B	W	I
Y	V	G	A	Y	A	M	U	N	A	H	S
A	B	B	A	S	D	F	G	H	J	K	L
B	R	A	H	M	A	P	U	T	R	A	F